# HE
# REIGNS

Published in 2023 by Kingdom Faith Church
Foundry Lane, Horsham, West Sussex, RH13 5PX, UK.
www.kingdomfaith.com

ISBN 978-1-9163282-1-1

**A 21 DAY DEVOTIONAL
ON THE COMING KING**

# Contents

# Introduction

When I was thinking of whether to write a book these words came to mind:

'Publish and proclaim peace and the good news of salvation, And tell Zion, "Your God reigns!"' (Isaiah 52:7)

This devotional is written from one of the most beautiful promises of God in Isaiah chapter 9 of how He would send the Messiah to His people Israel. He would step into the intense darkness of this world to rescue and bring relief from suffering, and establish His reign in the earth.

The Wonderful Counsellor, Mighty God, Everlasting Father and Prince of Peace came to establish His reign for Jew and Gentile alike, both now and in the glorious Kingdom to come!

What wonderful hope and reassurance in these uncertain times.

I felt to write this as a devotional so that each day you can immerse yourself in God's Word. Then spend time abiding, dwelling and meditating on what it means for you and then respond in prayer. God wants you to KNOW that He reigns, that He has overcome, and that He is in control. His reign is for your life now and He has a wonderful inheritance for you to come!

There is an invitation each day to -

**Abide** - rest and dwell in His love for you and His finished work.

**Align** - your heart and mind to His wonderful Word. Where there is agreement and alignment with Truth it brings harmony and peace to your heart, mind and body.

**Apply** - His overcoming victory and reign in your life.

Enjoy x

For all those who
long for His coming.

# The Coming Messiah

But in the midst of judgment there is the promise
and the certainty of the Lord's deliverance
and there shall be no gloom for her who was in
anguish. In the former time the Lord brought
into contempt the land of Zebulun and the land
of Naphtali, but in the latter time He will make it
glorious, by the way of the Sea of Galilee, the land
beyond the Jordan, Galilee of the nations.

The people who walked in darkness have seen a
great Light; those who dwelt in the land of intense
darkness and the shadow of death, upon them
has the Light shined.

You O Lord have multiplied the nation and
increased their joy; they rejoice before You like the
joy in harvest, as men rejoice when they divide
the spoil of battle.

For the yoke of Israel's burden, and the staff or rod for goading their shoulders, the rod of their oppressor, You have broken as in the day of Gideon with Midian.

For every tramping warrior's war boots and all his armour in the battle tumult and every garment rolled in blood shall be burned as fuel for the fire.

For to us a Child is born, to us a Son is given; and the government shall be upon His shoulder, and His name shall be called Wonderful Counsellor, Mighty God, Everlasting Father of Eternity, Prince of Peace.

Of the increase of His government and of peace there shall be no end, upon the throne of David and over His kingdom, to establish it and to uphold it with justice and with righteousness from the latter time forth, even forevermore. The zeal of the Lord of hosts will perform this.

Isaiah 9:1-7 (AMPC)

In the midst of judgement there is the promise and the certainty of the Lord's deliverance and there shall be no gloom for her who was in anguish.

Isaiah 9:1 (AMPC)

# Day 1

*Reconciled*

This is an amazing promise from God for His people Israel. God had chosen them to walk with Him and know Him and made a covenant with them that they would be a blessed nation and a blessing to the nations. However, in their struggle to walk with God and in their sin, they were now living under judgement and oppression from their enemies. So God, in His love and mercy, determined to intervene and deliver them.

He would send the Messiah (Christ), the Saviour, who would take on the judgement they deserved. Formerly their sin was covered by the blood sacrifice of an animal but the Messiah would give himself as a sacrifice, shed his blood, to bring their deliverance and freedom.

Isaiah prophesied the coming Messiah as the suffering servant of His people:

"He was despised and rejected—
   a Man of sorrows, acquainted with deepest grief.
We turned our backs on Him and looked the other way.
   He was despised, and we did not care.
Yet it was our weaknesses He carried;
   it was our sorrows that weighed Him down.
And we thought His troubles were a punishment from God,
   a punishment for His own sins!
But He was pierced for our rebellion,
   crushed for our sins.
He was beaten so we could be whole.
   He was whipped so we could be healed.
All of us, like sheep, have strayed away.
   We have left God's paths to follow our own.
Yet the Lord laid on Him
   the sins of us all.
He was oppressed and treated harshly,
   yet He never said a word.
He was led like a lamb to the slaughter.
   And as a sheep is silent before the shearers,
   He did not open His mouth.
Unjustly condemned,
   He was led away.
No one cared that He died without descendants,

that His life was cut short in midstream.
But He was struck down
  for the rebellion of my people.
He had done no wrong
  and had never deceived anyone.
But He was buried like a criminal;
  He was put in a rich man's grave.
But it was the Lord's good plan to crush Him
  and cause Him grief.
Yet when His life is made an offering for sin,
  He will have many descendants.
He will enjoy a long life,
  and the Lord's good plan will prosper in His hands.
When He sees all that is accomplished by His anguish,
  He will be satisfied."
- Isaiah 53:3-11

The Messiah, Jesus, came and died the cruel death of crucifixion not just for Israel but for all mankind; for Jew and Gentile alike. He died once and for all.

**What love, what mercy!**

"For God in all His fullness
  was pleased to live in Christ,
and through Him God reconciled
  everything to Himself.

He made peace with everything in heaven and on earth
  by means of Christ's blood on the cross."
- Colossians 1:19-20

To be reconciled means to be made "at one" with God. Reconciliation is atonement (at-one-ment). Reconciliation means having a relationship and peace with God where once there was separation.[1] God has been pleased and satisfied, through the Messiah's sacrifice of His perfect life for our imperfect life, to reconcile us to Himself forever.

## What a beautiful exchange!

There is now available to us forgiveness of our sins when we ask Him to forgive us. He took on Himself our sicknesses and by the wounds He suffered we can receive healing. Through His wonderful mercy His blood shed for us makes us clean. The extreme mental, emotional and physical distress and anguish that He went through in our place means we can be made whole in every way and live free!

**Selah...pause**

Abide...

in His love and mercy toward you that is sure and certain.

..................................................................................................................

..................................................................................................................

Align...

with the truth that the Messiah's sacrifice has delivered you
and has reconciled you to God.

..................................................................................................................

..................................................................................................................

Apply...

ask Him to forgive your sin and heal and deliver you from
sickness and anguish in your life.

..................................................................................................................

..................................................................................................................

Thank you, Lord, that I can now live in the freedom and
healing that You have been pleased to give me!

"There may be some sins of which a man cannot speak, but there is no sin which the blood of Christ cannot wash away."

Charles Spurgeon

If we confess our sins,
He is faithful and
just and will forgive
us our sins and
purify us from all
unrighteousness.

1 John 1:9 (NIV)

In the former time
the Lord brought into
contempt the land of
Zebulun and the land
of Naphtali, but in the
latter time He will
make it glorious,
by the way of the
Sea of Galilee.

Isaiah 9:1 (AMPC)

# Day 2

*Glory*

God's wonderful intention was always for His people Israel to know Him, to walk with Him and live an abundant, blessed life under His reign. They were to be a witness to other nations of God's glory - His goodness and faithfulness - to His people.

His deliverance for them would restore His glory and honour to them so they could live in His abundant goodness once more - not because they deserved it but because He loved them!

"The Lord did not set His heart on you and choose you because you were more numerous than other nations, for you were the smallest of all nations! Rather, it was simply that the Lord loves you, and He was keeping the oath He had sworn to your ancestors." - Deuteronomy 7:7-8

The glory of God was seen in His love, faithfulness and mercy towards His people Israel. They experienced His glorious presence and holiness in the temple. God was glorified in majesty in the incredible miracles worked on their behalf. Others were in awe of the blessings Israel lived under because of His eternal love towards them (1 Kings 10).

Israel's king David wrote this in recognition of God's wonderful kindness to His people:

"O Lord, the God of our ancestor Israel, may you be praised forever and ever! Yours, O Lord, is the greatness, the power, the glory, the victory, and the majesty. Everything in the heavens and on earth is Yours, O Lord, and this is Your Kingdom. We adore You as the One who is over all things. Wealth and honour come from You alone, for You rule over everything. Power and might are in Your hand, and at Your discretion people are made great and given strength. O God, We thank and praise Your glorious name." - 1 Chronicles 29:10-13

God's faithfulness to His Word and to His people meant sending the Messiah from the glorious presence of God to dwell among them. He came demonstrating the glorious Kingdom of God in His goodness, miracles, victory, and power - His reign on earth as it is in heaven! His glory and honour are now our inheritance. His reign in our lives will make us glorious!

# We are His glorious inheritance!

These are two wonderful truths about you now...

"He lifts the poor from the dust
  and the needy from the garbage dump.
He sets them among princes,
  placing them in seats of honour.
For all the earth is the Lord's,
  and He has set the world in order."
- 1 Samuel 2:8

"Arise, shine, for your light has come,
  and the glory of the Lord rises upon you.
See, darkness covers the earth
  and thick darkness is over the peoples,
but the Lord rises upon you
  and His glory appears over you.
Nations will come to your light,
  and kings to the brightness of your dawn."
- Isaiah 60:1-3 (NIV)

**Selah...pause**

**Abide...**

*in God's love and goodness toward you.*

.................................................................................................

.................................................................................................

.................................................................................................

**Align...**

*with the truth that you are made for His glory and honour.*

.................................................................................................

.................................................................................................

.................................................................................................

**Apply...**

*ask Him to fill you with His glory.*

.................................................................................................

.................................................................................................

.................................................................................................

*Thank you, Lord, that You have made me glorious.*
*I can arise and shine!*

For how great
is God's goodness
And how great
is His beauty
And how great He will
make Israel's goodness
And how great He will
make Israel's beauty.

Zechariah 9:17

You will Glory
in the Holy One
of Israel.

Isaiah 41:16

The people who
walked in darkness
have seen a great
Light; those who dwelt
in the land of intense
darkness and the
shadow of death,
upon them has the
Light shined.

Isaiah 9:2 (AMPC)

# Day 3
## Redemption

When the Messiah came to His people Israel two thousand years ago and walked the land of Judea, the light of His life broke through the darkness.

When asked if He was the Messiah that the people had been waiting for, He simply replied: "Go back and tell them 'what you have seen and heard—the blind see, the lame walk, those with leprosy are cured, the deaf hear, the dead are raised to life, and the Good News is being preached to the poor.'"
- Luke 7:22

All these were signs; proof that God's reign and glorious Kingdom had come. His goodness in action and His power available for all who would come to Him.

But it wasn't until the Cross that our redemption came. The Good News is more than healing, miracles and deliverance from demons. The Good News is redemption. The Good News is that the Messiah died and shed His blood to pay the price for our sins and to redeem us back to God. When He cried "It is finished," it really was!

Redemption means to gain or regain possession of something in exchange for payment.[2] "The thief's purpose is to steal and kill and destroy. My purpose," said the Messiah "is to give you a rich and satisfying life" (John 10:10 AMPC).

What mercy and love that the Messiah came into the intense darkness and depravity of the world to break the power of sin, depression, loss and hurt in our lives. Not only that, but when He rose from the dead after three days He had overcome death - it had no power over Him!

He is our victorious, risen King who now reigns over all, with all the authority of heaven and earth. He can say, "Do not be afraid, I am the Alpha and Omega, the beginning and the end, I hold the keys of death and hell" - Revelation 1:18. He really does have the last word!

*It is finished!*

When you put your faith in Him, in His finished work of the

cross, we no longer need to walk in darkness. We no longer need to live in fear of death or destruction. He took our sorrows and experienced our deepest grief. There is no curse, no demonic power, no trauma, no evil that can overcome us. No shadow of shame, guilt, regret, fear, disappointment, anger or anxiety can consume us. His light has come!

We no longer live in darkness or under shadows, we live in His Light under His wonderful reign!

"Those who live in the shelter of the Most High
  will find rest in the shadow of the Almighty.
This I declare about the Lord:
He alone is my refuge, my place of safety;
  He is my God, and I trust Him.
For He will rescue you from every trap
  and protect you from deadly disease.
He will cover you with His feathers.
  He will shelter you with His wings.
  His faithful promises are your armour and protection.
Do not be afraid of the terrors of the night,
  nor the arrow that flies in the day.
Do not dread the disease that stalks in darkness,
  nor the disaster that strikes at midday.
Though a thousand fall at your side,
  though ten thousand are dying around you,
  these evils will not touch you.

Just open your eyes,
  and see how the wicked are punished.
If you make the Lord your refuge,
  if you make the Most High your shelter,
no evil will conquer you;
  no plague will come near your home.
For He will order His angels
  to protect you wherever you go.
They will hold you up with their hands
  so you won't even hurt your foot on a stone.
You will trample upon lions and cobras;
  you will crush fierce lions and serpents under your feet!
The Lord says, 'I will rescue those who love Me.
  I will protect those who trust in My name.
When they call on Me, I will answer;
  I will be with them in trouble.
  I will rescue and honour them.
I will reward them with a long life
  and give them My salvation.'"
- Psalm 91:1-11,14-16

Selah...pause

**Abide...**
under the shadow of His wings.

.........................................................................................................

.........................................................................................................

**Align...**
to the truth that darkness is removed by His Light.

.........................................................................................................

.........................................................................................................

**Apply...**
ask Him to remove every trace of darkness or shadows in
your life and fill you with His Light.

.........................................................................................................

.........................................................................................................

Thank you, Lord, that You paid the price for me, Your blood
covered me "I am redeemed, it is finished!"

How precious is Your
unfailing love, O God!
All humanity
finds shelter in the
shadow of Your wings.
You feed them from
the abundance of Your

own house,

letting them drink
from Your river
of delights.
For You are the
fountain of life,
the light by which
we see.

Psalm 36:7-8

You, O Lord,
have multiplied
the nation...

Isaiah 9:3

# Day 4

## Restoration

From creation, the very beginning where God breathed life into man, God's desire was for man to walk with Him, in close communion and relationship with Him. To live with His presence and His purpose! We were to multiply and increase and fill the earth (Genesis 1:28) with His authority, power and love. This was to be our destiny - to reign with Him.

We lost this identity and inheritance with God when man believed the lie of the enemy causing him to doubt God's goodness. This led to him acting independently of God which is sin. This caused separation from God. However, God would choose another man to walk with. He chose Abraham who walked with God in faithfulness and God blessed him and said that He would be Abraham's shield and very great reward (Genesis 15:1) a wonderful promise of protection and provision! He gave Abraham and his descendants a promise that through them would come a people who would walk with God, know Him and be a blessing to all the nations of the earth.

"For you (Israel) are a holy people, who belong to the Lord your God. Of all the people on earth, the Lord your God has chosen you to be His own special treasure...Understand, therefore, that the Lord your God is indeed God. He is the faithful God who keeps His covenant for a thousand generations and lavishes His unfailing love on those who love Him and obey His commands...He will love you and bless you, and He will give you many children. He will give fertility to your land and your animals.

*Now! God wants to lavish His people with His love.*

God is not a small God. He does not want restriction, small thinking, loss or depletion in our lives. He wants us to increase and multiply, to fill the earth. Unfortunately, the people of Israel struggled to walk with God. Instead of walking in their calling to bless the nations, they lost everything. And so the Messiah came to buy back what was lost and restore what was taken. He would restore their inheritance and their calling so that they could live His Kingdom life on earth.

Restoration can be defined as the act of returning something to its former condition; to make something new again; to bring back into use something that has been absent for a period of time; to give something that has been lost or stolen back to the person it belongs to.[3]

When we believe what He has done and ask Him to be Lord we step into our rightful inheritance and destiny - Kingdom life full of His goodness and abundance. We are now a people of a different spirit and occupy our homes and communities with His ways. The restoration of our relationship with God brings security, a sense of purpose and a good future! He restores dignity and our sense of self worth. This enables restoration in our relationships with others that may have been lost or broken.

"After you have suffered a little while, the God of all grace who has called you to His eternal glory will Himself restore, confirm, strengthen and establish you." - 1 Peter 5:10 (ESV)

God is a generational God who works through families, so He blesses us with children/descendants physically and/ or spiritually where we help the next generation to know Him and His ways. Restoration can enable gifts and talents that have maybe lain dormant or pushed aside in us to come alive. With healing mentally, emotionally or physically, our capacity to create or work increases and we find ourselves accomplishing more than we ever dreamed of!

## *Increase is coming!*

"Enlarge the place of your tent,
   stretch your tent curtains wide,
   do not hold back;
lengthen your cords,
   strengthen your stakes.
For you will spread out to the right and to the left;
   your descendants will dispossess nations
   and settle in their desolate cities.
Do not be afraid; you will not be put to shame.
   Do not fear disgrace; you will not be humiliated.
You will forget the shame of your youth
   and remember no more the reproach of your widowhood.
For your Maker is your husband –
   the Lord Almighty is His name –
the Holy One of Israel is your Redeemer;
   He is called the God of all the earth."
- Isaiah 54:2-5 (NIV)

**Selah...pause**

**Abide...**

*in His love that He lavishes on you!*

......................................................................................................................

......................................................................................................................

**Align...**

*with the truth of His restoration and increased blessings in your life.*

......................................................................................................................

......................................................................................................................

**Apply...**

*ask Him to release you from any restriction in your life and to bring the increase that He has.*

......................................................................................................................

......................................................................................................................

*Thank you, Lord, that I can live in an inheritance with You and reign in life as You always intended!*

For now it will be said of Jacob, 'What wonders God has done for Israel!'

Numbers 23:23

"You will never cease to be the most amazed person on earth at what God has done for you on the inside."

Oswald Chambers

...and increased
its joy

Isaiah 9:3

# Day 5

*Joy*

God wants His people living in joy.

Right standing with God brings overwhelming joy where we used to be overwhelmed at life! "I am overwhelmed with joy in the Lord my God. For He has dressed me with the clothing of salvation and draped me in a robe of righteousness." - Psalm 61:10

This is such a beautiful verse and a beautiful picture!

We have been clothed in His beautiful gifts to us of salvation and righteousness. What joy there is for us when there is reconciliation with God and restoration of all that was lost! What overwhelming joy comes with deliverance from darkness and deliverance from sin and judgement. How amazing and how different from mere religion.

True restoration in our relationship with God brings a new identity that brings deep joy. We have been forgiven, delivered and healed from wounds of trauma and pain. We have been beautified by Him. We can live in a new sense of freedom knowing He has robed us in righteousness and honour - we can live with hope for better days.

God's joy in us is made up of His great delight towards us. Don't be grieved or depressed, "for the joy of the Lord is your strength and stronghold!" - Nehemiah 8:10 (AMPC). It's His joy about us, towards us and in us that keeps us strong - of course we can walk tall when we realise He delights in us!

It gives Him great joy that we can now come into His presence and experience His fullness of joy. That's why He came. For the joy set before Jesus He went to the cross, He endured its shame, humiliation and horror knowing salvation for us would be on the other side, that we could then come into His presence and be with Him forever (Hebrews 12:2).

"Instead of shame and dishonour,
   you will enjoy a double share of honour.
You will possess a double portion of prosperity in your land,
   and everlasting joy will be yours."
- Isaiah 61:7

This is true joy. He bore our shame and the one who believes in Him will never be put to shame. We have complete freedom from shame and a whole new inheritance of honour and joy. Where life may have been a struggle, we may have lived under a cloud and been facing each day with dread, now through faith in Him, joy and honour are ours.

*Inexpressible joy filled with glory!*

And this is our faith. "Though you have not seen Him, you love Him. Though you do not now see Him, you believe in Him and rejoice with joy that is inexpressible and filled with glory." - 1 Peter 1:8-9 (ESV)

**Selah...pause**

**Abide...**

*in His fullness of joy toward you!*

........................................................................................................

........................................................................................................

........................................................................................................

**Align...**

*with the truth that He has released you from trauma and pain through His acceptance of you.*

........................................................................................................

........................................................................................................

........................................................................................................

**Apply...**

*ask Him to heal every negative emotion and shame and to overwhelm you with His love and joy.*

........................................................................................................

........................................................................................................

........................................................................................................

Thank you, Lord, that I can be satisfied every day with You and be full of deep joy.

May you be filled
with joy, always
thanking the Father.
He has enabled
you to share in
the inheritance that
belongs to His people,
who live in the light.

Colossians 1:12

In Your presence
there is fullness
of joy.

Psalm 16:11 (ESV)

They will rejoice before You as people rejoice at the harvest and like warriors dividing the plunder.

Isaiah 9:3

# Day 6

## Sing!

"Oh that the salvation and deliverance of Israel would come out of Zion! When God restores the fortunes of His people, then will Jacob rejoice and Israel be glad." - Psalm 53:6 (AMPC)

On Mount Zion, as promised, the Messiah bought back His people and made them acceptable to God! He restored their calling and identity. They can now come to Him in boldness and confidence and full of joy. No wonder they rejoice before Him, their faithful God and deliverer.

"How could I be silent when it's time to praise You? Now my heart sings out, bursting with joy—a bliss inside that keeps me singing, 'I can never thank You enough!'"
- Psalm 30:12 (TPT)

What a wonderful verse. With salvation, deliverance, and a new life made available for us all, we can never thank Him enough! Constant thankfulness to God shows our deep gratitude for what He has done for us. For saving us, changing our lives and restoring our fortunes He is worthy of all our praise.

If we don't sing His praises, who else will?! For You are now a "chosen people, a royal priesthood, a holy nation, God's special possession, that you may declare the praises of Him who called you out of darkness into His wonderful light" - 1 Peter 2:9 (NIV). Where there was once one priest from God's people who would minister to God we are now all a priesthood, His special people to declare His praises continually. We join with the whole host of heaven that is in adoration and worship of God day and night declaring He is worthy.

*We can bring Him extravagant worship!*

There's an amazing story where Jesus heals ten lepers but out of the ten only one turns to Jesus to thank Him. "Then one of them, upon seeing that he was cured, turned back, recognizing and thanking and praising God with a loud voice; And he fell prostrate at Jesus' feet, thanking Him [over and over]. And he was a Samaritan. Then Jesus asked, Were not [all] ten cleansed? Where are the nine?" - Luke 17:15-17 (AMPC)

The way this leper thanked Jesus shows such overwhelming gratitude for his healing - he didn't hold back. And where were the others? Jesus wondered that also! Our thankfulness, our acknowledgement, our praise and worship are important to Him. They are our heart and faith responses.

"Songs of joy and victory are sung in the camp of the godly.
   The strong right arm of the Lord has done glorious things!
The strong right arm of the Lord is raised in triumph.
   The strong right arm of the Lord has done glorious things!
I will not die; instead, I will live
   to tell what the Lord has done."
- Psalm 118:15-17

*I will live to tell of Your wonderful acts!*

This is an amazing truth! He saved our lives from the destruction we were heading into. No wonder we can sing and declare that our God reigns, declare that our God is mighty to save.

When we sing and proclaim the truth of who He is, it shifts atmospheres! God is lifted up and moves through our praise and declarations! The enemy and dark forces are pushed back through proclamations of who He is. We release the victory sound of heaven as we make a joyful noise on the earth!

"Let the whole earth sing to the Lord!
  Each day proclaim the good news that He saves.
Publish His glorious deeds among the nations.
  Tell everyone about the amazing things He does.
Great is the Lord! He is most worthy of praise!
  He is to be feared above all gods.
The gods of other nations are mere idols,
  but the Lord made the heavens!
Honour and majesty surround Him;
  strength and joy fill His dwelling.

O nations of the world, recognize the Lord,
  recognize that the Lord is glorious and strong.
Give to the Lord the glory He deserves!
  Bring your offering and come into His presence.
Worship the Lord in all His holy splendour.
  Let all the earth tremble before Him.
  The world stands firm and cannot be shaken.

Let the heavens be glad, and the earth rejoice!
  Tell all the nations, 'The Lord reigns!'"
- 1 Chronicles 16:23-30

**Selah...pause**

Abide...
*Worship Him - He is worthy!*

Align...
*With the truth that you can come boldly and confidently into His presence.*

Apply...
*I praise You, Lord, that I will live and I will be thankful everyday and tell others what You have done!*

Come let us
adore Him.

Shout aloud and sing
for joy, people of
Zion, for great is the
Holy One of Israel
among you.

Isaiah 12:6 (NIV)

For You will break
the yoke of their
slavery and lift the
heavy burden from
their shoulders.

Isaiah 9:4

# Day 7

## He has broken the Yoke

The Messiah, Jesus, came to break the burden (yoke) of sin and the heavy religious burden that His people lived under. He lived God's laws perfectly, obeyed them perfectly and then fulfilled them by being the perfect sacrifice for sin, once and for all. All record of sin is cancelled, the charge against us was nailed to the cross (Colossians 2:14). There is now no condemnation, no one needs to strive to be righteous. He is our righteousness!

Jesus now encourages us to come to Him. "Come to Me, all you who labour and are heavy-laden and overburdened, and I will cause you to rest. I will ease and relieve and refresh your souls. Take My yoke upon you and learn of Me, for I am gentle (meek) and humble (lowly) in heart, and you will find rest,

relief and ease and refreshment and recreation and blessed quiet for your souls. For My yoke is wholesome, useful, good—not harsh, hard, sharp, or pressing, but comfortable, gracious, and pleasant and My burden is light and easy to be borne."
- Matthew 11:28-30 (AMPC)

*What a beautiful invitation!*

He carried the heavy wooden cross (yoke) on His shoulders and took the weight of our sin so we are free and can come to Him. He is gentle and encourages us to rise up and stand up. "Arise from the depression and prostration in which circumstances have kept you—rise to a new life!" - Isaiah 60:1 (AMPC). Wow! We are actually released from depression and oppression, everything that has weighed heavy on us, that enslaved us and held us down.

"Wake up, wake up, O Zion!
   Clothe yourself with strength.
Put on your beautiful clothes, O holy city of Jerusalem,
   for unclean and godless people will enter your gates no longer
Rise from the dust, O Jerusalem.
   Sit in a place of honour.
Remove the chains of slavery from your neck,
   O captive daughter of Zion."
- Isaiah 52:1-2.

This is such a beautiful picture of His people being free now! We wake up to what He has done and who we are. We can remove all chains of slavery! We are free to rise up from the dust, sit in a place of honour and put on royal garments of splendour. This is truly amazing!

There are many chains and burdens we live under, but fear is one of the most common and most debilitating. That's why God said to His people so often: "Do not fear!"

"But as for you, Israel My servant,
  Jacob My chosen one,
  descended from Abraham My friend,
I have called you back from the ends of the earth,
  saying, 'You are My servant.'
For I have chosen you
  and will not throw you away.
Don't be afraid, for I am with you.
  Don't be discouraged, for I am your God.
I will strengthen you and help you.
  I will hold you up with My victorious right hand.
See, all your angry enemies lie there,
  confused and humiliated.
Anyone who opposes you will die
  and come to nothing.
You will look in vain
  for those who tried to conquer you.

Those who attack you
  will come to nothing.
For I hold you by your right hand—
  I, the Lord your God.
And I say to you,
  'Don't be afraid. I am here to help you.
Though you are a lowly worm, O Jacob,
  don't be afraid, people of Israel, for I will help you.
I am the Lord, your Redeemer.
  I am the Holy One of Israel'...
Then you will rejoice in the Lord.
  You will glory in the Holy One of Israel."
- Isaiah 41:8-14,16

"Do not be afraid, for I have ransomed you. I have called you by name; you are Mine...you are precious to Me. You are honoured and I love you. Do not be afraid for I am with you."
- Isaiah 43:1,4-5

He has broken the power of fear and delivered us from it! We are now His. He wants us to trust His rule and reign in our lives. We no longer have a spirit of fear, "but of power, love and a sound mind!" - 2 Timothy 1:7 (NKJV)

**Selah...pause**

**Abide...**

come to Him and let Him give you rest.

........................................................................................................................

........................................................................................................................

**Align...**

with the truth that every burden of depression, oppression and fear is broken.

........................................................................................................................

........................................................................................................................

**Apply...**

ask Him to take every heavy burden off you and enable you to arise to a new life.

........................................................................................................................

........................................................................................................................

Thank you, Lord, that I can rise up to a new life. I do not have a spirit of fear, but of power, love and a sound mind - Your wonderful thoughts toward me!

Let me be clear the Anointed One has set us free – not partially but completely and wonderfully free! We must always cherish this truth and stubbornly refuse to go back to the bondage of our past!

Galatians 5:1 (TPT)

May those who love
you rise like the sun
in all its power.

Judges 5:31

You will break the
oppressor's rod, just
as You did when You
destroyed the army
of Midian.

Isaiah 9:4

# Day 8
## The Shepherd of Israel

The rod and staff were used by shepherds to guide sheep, to direct them away from danger and lead them to safe places to graze. In the Old Testament, God called Himself the Shepherd of Israel and the people His sheep (Psalm 80:1). When the people of Israel strayed from God, they lived under oppression or even scattered from their land.

God promised that He would search for them, bring them home and care for them once more under His reign.

"For this is what the Sovereign Lord says: I Myself will search and find My sheep. I will be like a shepherd looking for his scattered flock. I will find My sheep and rescue them from all the places where they were scattered on that dark and

cloudy day. I will bring them back home to their own land of Israel from among the peoples and nations. I will feed them on the mountains of Israel and by the rivers and in all the places where people live. Yes, I will give them good pastureland on the high hills of Israel. There they will lie down in pleasant places and feed in the lush pastures of the hills. I Myself will tend My sheep and give them a place to lie down in peace, says the Sovereign Lord. I will search for my lost ones who strayed away, and I will bring them safely home again. I will bandage the injured and strengthen the weak...In this way, they will know that I, the Lord their God, am with them. And they will know that they, the people of Israel, are My people, says the Sovereign Lord. You are My flock, the sheep of My pasture. You are My people, and I am your God. I, the Sovereign Lord, have spoken!"
- Ezekiel 34:11-16,30-31

What a beautiful promise of God! He would gather His people back to Himself and to their land. He would send the Messiah, Jesus, as the Good Shepherd. Jesus said: "I came for the lost sheep of Israel" (Matthew 15:24). They are "like sheep without a shepherd" (Matthew 9:36). "I am the Good Shepherd. The Good Shepherd lays down His life for the sheep....I lay down My life for the sheep" (John 10:11,15).

When He laid down His life on the cross, He triumphed over the enemy. He broke the enemy's rod, his hold over all mankind, so that we could follow Him instead. We can live under His wonderful reign.

## The Lord is my shepherd!

Psalm 23 is a beautiful picture of what the Good Shepherd does for His people.

"The Lord is my Shepherd [to feed, guide, and shield me], I shall not lack. He makes me lie down in [fresh, tender] green pastures; He leads me beside the still and restful waters. He refreshes and restores my life (my self); He leads me in the paths of righteousness [uprightness and right standing with Him—not for my earning it, but] for His name's sake. Yes, though I walk through the [deep, sunless] valley of the shadow of death, I will fear or dread no evil, for You are with me; Your rod [to protect] and Your staff [to guide], they comfort me. You prepare a table before me in the presence of my enemies. You anoint my head with oil; my [brimming] cup runs over. Surely or only goodness, mercy, and unfailing love shall follow me all the days of my life, and through the length of my days the house of the Lord [and His presence] shall be my dwelling place." - Psalm 23 (AMPC)

If we follow Jesus, our Good Shepherd, we can trust that He will guide us through life, leading us through every season in His mercy, comfort, strength and protection. He will take care of us and meet every need with His abundance! He leads us to His table, His presence, the place where He has prepared a feast for us, and we will feast on His goodness forever. The enemy cannot touch us. The rod and staff not only guide His people but He also uses them to destroy His enemies! God's presence and His reign is our safe place just as He always intended!


**Selah...pause**

**Abide...**

*dwell in His loving care as Your Shepherd.*

...................................................................................................................................

...................................................................................................................................

**Align...**

*to the truth that He only has the best for you and you can trust His leading of your life.*

...................................................................................................................................

...................................................................................................................................

**Apply...**

*ask Him to lead and guide you through every high and low and determine to stay close to Him!*

...................................................................................................................................

...................................................................................................................................

*Thank you, Lord that You are faithful to lead me through life, with goodness and mercy following, to a glorious destiny!*

"My sheep listen to My voice; I know them, and they follow Me. I give them eternal life, and they shall never perish; no one can snatch them out of My hand."

John 10:27–28

There is no one like the God of Israel.
He rides across the heavens to help you,
across the skies in majestic splendour.
The eternal God is your refuge,
and His everlasting arms are under you.
He drives out the enemy before you;
He cries out, 'Destroy them!'
So Israel will live in safety,
prosperous Jacob in security,
in a land of grain and new wine,
while the heavens drop down dew.
How blessed you are, O Israel!
Who else is like you,
a people saved by the Lord?
He is your protecting shield
and your triumphant sword!

Deuteronomy 33:26-29

The boots of
the warrior and
the uniforms
bloodstained by war
will all be burned.
They will be fuel for
the fire.

Isaiah 9:5

# Day 9

## His Victorious Reign

When God speaks to His people prophetically in the Bible it can be understood on different levels. Isaiah 9 speaks of the Messiah coming and delivering His people spiritually out of darkness but it also speaks of a time in the future when He will rule and reign as King over His people Israel and the whole earth.

"He shall judge between the nations,
   and shall decide disputes for many peoples;
and they shall beat their swords into plowshares,
   and their spears into pruning hooks;
nation shall not lift up sword against nation,
   neither shall they learn war anymore."
- Isaiah 2:4 (ESV)

The United Nations has the last part of this verse as their motto, but only when the Messiah comes to rule and reign on the earth in the future will wars end between nations. God is a consuming fire, He will judge the nations and deal with His enemies forever.

On the cross, the Messiah's sacrifice destroyed the power of sin and its effects from our lives. God loved us and gave Himself up for us as a fragrant offering and sacrifice to God (Ephesians 5:2 ESV). Every warring thing in us and against us has been burned up.

*He truly redeems everything!*

These amazing verses in Isaiah 61 explain what Jesus has done. He makes all things new! Believe what He has done for you!

"The Spirit of the Lord God is upon me, because the Lord has anointed and qualified me to preach the Gospel of good tidings to the meek, the poor, and afflicted; He has sent me to bind up and heal the brokenhearted, to proclaim liberty to the captives and the opening of the prison and of the eyes to those who are bound, To proclaim the acceptable year of the Lord [the year of His favour] and the day of vengeance of our God, to comfort all who mourn, To grant [consolation and joy] to those who mourn in Zion—to give them an ornament (a garland or diadem) of beauty instead of ashes, the oil of

joy instead of mourning, the garment [expressive] of praise instead of a heavy, burdened, and failing spirit—that they may be called oaks of righteousness [lofty, strong, and magnificent, distinguished for uprightness, justice, and right standing with God], the planting of the Lord, that He may be glorified."
- Isaiah 61:1-3 (AMPC)

Wow. This is good news! There is healing for every area of our lives. He makes all things new and He now enables us to live as overcomers.  Isaiah 61 goes on to say 'And they shall rebuild the ancient ruins; they shall raise up the former desolations and renew the ruined cities, the devastations of many generations...you shall be called the priests of the Lord; people will speak of you as the ministers of our God." - Isaiah 61:4,6

This is now who we are. The past has become fuel for the fire going forward! Where destruction and devastation were at work in our lives, even in past generations of our families, now new life has come. We now build a new future for ourselves and for others for generations to come! He shows loving devotion to a thousand generations of those who love Him and keep His commandments (Exodus 20:6).

**Selah...pause**

**Abide...**

*in His complete healing for you.*

........................................................................................

........................................................................................

........................................................................................

**Align...**

*with the truth that the battle is over; the old has gone and the new has come.*

........................................................................................

........................................................................................

........................................................................................

**Apply...**

*ask Him to heal every area of your life, even your broken heart, and to make all things new.*

........................................................................................

........................................................................................

........................................................................................

*Thank you, Lord, for healing me and making me stand strong, magnificent and distinguished — I will live to bring Your victorious reign to others.*

We overcome by the
blood of the lamb
and the word of
our testimony.

Revelation 12:11 (NKJV)

*Beauty for ashes.*

Isaiah 61:3

# For a Child is born to us...

Isaiah 9:6

# Day 10

## *Immanuel*

God spoke to the prophet Isaiah twice that He would come to save the people of Israel through a Child being born. "The Lord Himself will give you the sign. Look! The virgin will conceive a Child! She will give birth to a Son and will call Him Immanuel (which means 'God with us')." - Isaiah 7:14

Seven hundred years later, the angel Gabriel visited the virgin Mary. The angel told her, "Don't be afraid... for you have found favour with God! You will conceive and give birth to a Son, and you will name Him Jesus. He will be very great and will be called the Son of the Most High. The Lord God will give Him the throne of His ancestor David. And He will reign over Israel forever; His Kingdom will never end!" - Luke 1:30-33

Joseph, the intended husband to Mary, was considering divorcing her secretly when "an angel of the Lord appeared to him in a dream. 'Joseph, son of David...do not be afraid to take Mary as your wife. For the Child within her was conceived by the Holy Spirit. And she will have a Son, and you are to name Him Jesus, for He will save His people from their sins.'"
- Matthew 1:20-21

God spoke many times through His prophets to His people of the details of the coming Messiah. The prophet Micah told of His birthplace:"But you, Bethlehem Ephrathah, though you are small among the clans of Judah, out of you will come for Me One who will be Ruler over Israel, whose origins are from of old, from ancient times." - Micah 5:2

The star that appeared at the Messiah's birth proclaiming that a ruler of Israel had been born was prophesied by Balaam, who saw it in an open vision way back in Israel's beginning.

"I see Him, but not here and now.
   I perceive Him, but far in the distant future.
A star will rise from Jacob;
   a sceptre will emerge from Israel."
- Numbers 24:17-18

He also said in that same prophecy that:

"God is not a man, so He does not lie.

He is not human, so He does not change His mind.
Has He ever spoken and failed to act?
Has He ever promised and not carried it through?
For the Lord their God is with them;
He has been proclaimed their King."
- Numbers 23:19,21

The star that was prophesied here was seen by the wise
Magi recorded in Matthew. They followed the rising star
that was telling of the birth of a king, asking, "Where is He
who has been born King of the Jews? For we have seen His
star in the east at its rising and have come to worship Him."
- Matthew 2:2

*He is proclaimed their King!*

That night there were shepherds staying in the fields nearby,
guarding their flocks of sheep. Suddenly, an angel of the Lord
appeared among them, and the radiance of the Lord's glory
surrounded them. They were terrified, but the angel reassured
them.

"Don't be afraid!" he said. "I bring you good news that will
bring great joy to all people. The Saviour—yes, the Messiah,
the Lord—has been born today in Bethlehem, the city of
David! And you will recognize Him by this sign: You will find
a Baby wrapped snugly in strips of cloth, lying in a manger."

Suddenly, the angel was joined by a vast host of others—the armies of heaven—praising God and saying,

"Glory to God in highest heaven,
  and peace on earth to those with whom God is pleased."
 - Luke 2:10-14

What wonderful news! He came as had been promised! He was born into our dark world in poverty to be like us and identify with us in every way. What good news of great joy. A King, Deliverer and Saviour has come to us! Immanuel!

**Selah...pause**

**Abide...**
in Immanuel, God with you.

..............................................................................................

..............................................................................................

**Align...**
with the truth that God is not a man that He should lie.

..............................................................................................

..............................................................................................

**Apply...**
ask God to remind you of any promises He has spoken over
your life that you haven't seen yet and remember that He is
faithful!

..............................................................................................

..............................................................................................

Thank you, Lord, that You can identify totally with my
humanity and yet You are the King who commands stars
and angels!

"Praise the Lord, the God of Israel, because He has visited and redeemed His people. He has sent us a mighty Saviour from the royal line of His servant David, just as He promised through His holy prophets long ago. Now we will be saved from our enemies and from all who hate us.

He has been merciful to our
ancestors by remembering
His sacred covenant - the
covenant He swore with
an oath to our ancestor
Abraham. We have been
rescued from our enemies
so we can serve God
without fear, in holiness
and righteousness for as
long as we live."

Luke 1:68-75

...a Son is
given to us

Isaiah 9:6

# Day 11
## The Son

The Son of God came to His people, Israel, who had waited so long for their Messiah.

As we have seen He was born a Hebrew, from the tribe of Judah, with genealogies proving His family line back to Abraham and David, He was circumcised on the eighth day and He was taken by His parents to the temple to be dedicated to the Lord. There was a man there named Simeon who had been waiting for the Messiah to come and rescue Israel. On seeing the Child, Jesus, he proclaimed: "I have seen Your salvation, which You have prepared for all people. He is a Light to reveal God to the nations, and He is the glory of Your people Israel!" - Luke 2:30-32

This is an amazing prophecy. Not only was the Son of God coming to be the glory of His people but also to reveal God to the Gentiles. For Jews, God was the Holy One of Israel! Yet here was a Jew proclaiming that the Messiah, the Son of God, had come to make God known to all, including idol worshipping pagans!

God's heart is that no one should perish so He came for the whole world.

"For God so loved the world that He gave His one and only Son, that whoever believes in Him shall not perish but have eternal life. For God did not send His Son into the world to condemn the world, but to save the world through Him. Whoever believes in Him is not condemned." - John 3:14–18 (NIV)

What beautiful verses. When we believe in His Son, Jew or Gentile, we are not condemned!

In the New Testament, God spoke audibly about Jesus: "This is My beloved Son with Him I am well pleased." - Matthew 3:17

And again He said: "This is My dearly loved Son who brings Me great joy, listen to Him." - Matthew 17:5

God spoke for all to hear, declaring that Jesus was His beloved Son. He wanted to get their attention! He wanted His people to know Him, believe in Him and love Him as He did! Jesus lived among them honouring the scriptures, the Sabbath, the feasts, and the Holy days. He brought God's love and Kingdom power with miracles of healing, of provision, and even raising the dead!

Jesus longed for them, weeping over Jerusalem, knowing they would reject Him. Many did believe but many did not. The Jewish people thought the Messiah would be a warrior King who would rid them of their enemy, the Romans! The religious Jews didn't believe God had a Son, so they had Jesus crucified as a heretic.

On the cross, Jesus cried: "Father forgive them for they know not what they do" - Luke 23:34. Right there His love overcame! He forgave them!

*What wonderful mercy and love!*

"God showed how much He loved us by sending His one and only Son into the world so that we might have eternal life through Him. This is real love, not that we loved God, but that He loved us and sent His Son as a sacrifice to take away our sins...We know how much God loves us, and we have put our trust in His love...We will not be afraid on the day of judgement but we can face Him with confidence." - 1 John 4:9-10,16,17

"God rescued us from the dominion of darkness
to bring us into the Kingdom of the Son He loves!"
- Colossians 1:13 (NIV)


**Selah...pause**

**Abide...**
in His perfect love, the same love He has for His Son!

**Align...**
with the truth that You are loved perfectly. This is a gift from God.

**Apply...**
ask Him to fill You with His love that you will not fear judgement.

Thank you, Lord, that You gave Your Son for Jew and Gentile alike. I will listen to Him and allow His reign in my life.

We know what real
love is because
Jesus gave up
His life for us.

1 John 3:16

So if the Son
sets you free,
you are truly
free.

John 8:36

The government
will rest on His
shoulders.

Isaiah 9:6

# Day 12

## His Government

The Hebrew word translated as "government" in Isaiah 9:6 means "dominion, power, or sovereignty through legal authority." [4]

Placing government on the shoulders speaks of royal authority. The government of the whole world now belongs to the Messiah, the Son of God! He overcame sin and death and rules and reigns with all legal authority!

All things in heaven and on the earth are now subject to Him. He ascended in triumph to be seated at the right hand of God, where He is crowned in splendour and majesty.

The prophet Daniel saw this:

"And to Him was given dominion
   and glory and a Kingdom,
that all peoples, nations, and languages
   should serve Him;
His dominion is an everlasting dominion,
   which shall not pass away,
and His Kingdom one
   that shall not be destroyed."
- Daniel 7:14 (ESV)

*He is not just Saviour but reigns as Lord and King!*

If we submit our lives to Him as our Lord, our lives are now under His rule and reign. We become disciples, not just converts! He wants His government to be in us and operating through us in this world. We listen to Him and submit to His authority. We align our lives to His teaching and honour His ways and we see His Kingdom released in our lives and to others. We seek first His Kingdom and His will in loving obedience.

"For this is the love of God, that we keep His commandments. And His commandments are not burdensome" - 1 John 5:3 (ESV)

We show our love for God through our obedience to Him.

"You are My friends if you do what I command." - John 15:14

Wow! Through our love and obedience to Him, He considers us His friends and wants to share with His people His plans and purposes.

"The friendship of the Lord is
  for those who fear Him,
    and He makes known to them His covenant. "
- Psalm 25:14 (ESV)

God is outworking His Kingdom government in the earth. He wants us to understand, have wisdom and be aware of what He is doing in our days.

"He changes times and seasons;
  He removes kings and sets up kings;
He gives wisdom to the wise
  and knowledge to those who have understanding."
- Daniel 2:21 (ESV)

Trusting God's governance enables us to stand firm in days of uncertainty and shaking. Jesus is seated at the right hand of God as our High Priest praying for us continually. He carries the weight of decisions, situations and circumstances for our lives and the nations!

We can lean on Him and bring Him our concerns and

questions, our worries and fears. We no longer need to carry the weight of the world on our shoulders. We can call on His name, on His power and on His wisdom.

We can trust His leading in these days, knowing He is in control and He will show us what we need to know and to do. To be like the men of Issachar, men who knew how to discern the times to know what Israel should do (1 Chronicles 12:32).

**Selah...pause**

**Abide...**

in your King.

................................................................................................................

................................................................................................................

**Align...**

with the truth that He is in control of your life and world events!

................................................................................................................

................................................................................................................

**Apply...**

surrender control of every area of your life to Him as a disciple living with His governance and Lordship.

................................................................................................................

................................................................................................................

Thank you, Lord, that I can walk as a disciple trusting Your wisdom and governance in the days we are in. You are on the throne!

For in Christ lives all the fullness of God in a human body. So you also are complete through your union with Christ, who is the head over every ruler and authority.

Colossians 2:9-10

Your promises are
backed by all the
honour of Your
name.


Psalm 138:2

And He will
be called...

Isaiah 9:6

# Day 13
## Who do you say I am?

This may be the most important question you will ever answer!

Jesus asked this question of the disciples. Referring to the crowds around them He asked, "Who do people say I am?" They replied, "some say John the Baptist, some say Elijah, and others say You are one of the other ancient prophets risen from the dead." Then He asked them, "But who do you say I am?"

Peter replied, "You are the Christ [the Messiah] God's Son, sent from God!"

Jesus replied, "On this rock, I will build My Church [My

ekklesia] and all the powers of hell cannot prevail against it and I will give you the keys of the Kingdom of heaven. Whatever you forbid on earth will be forbidden in heaven and whatever you permit on earth will be permitted in heaven." - Matthew 16:13-19

In other words, the understanding and revelation that Peter had, that Jesus was indeed the Messiah, the Son of God, is the foundational belief, the rock, that the Church is built upon and stands on. It is immovable. Whatever may have come against the Church over the centuries, it is still standing and still growing! It is part of a Kingdom that keeps advancing and no power from hell can stop it!

'The crowd,' then and now, may not understand who Jesus is or even want to know! The religious leaders hated Jesus for claiming He was sent from God. They had Jesus arrested and they sent Him to Pilate who asked Him if He was the King of the Jews.

Jesus replied, "My Kingdom is not an earthly kingdom...My Kingdom is not of this world."

Pilate said, "So You are a king?"

Jesus responded, "You say I am a king. Actually, I was born and came into the world to testify to the truth. All who love the truth recognize that what I say is true."

"What is truth?" Pilate asked. Then he went out again to the people and told them, "He is not guilty of any crime. But you have a custom of asking me to release one prisoner each year at Passover. Would you like me to release this 'King of the Jews'?" They said "No." - John 18:36-40

Many people don't believe that Jesus is the Saviour sent from God or don't want His truth. Some who do believe in Him may not want to align with His words; they don't want to live their lives according to His truth! We are in days where 'truth' is whatever people want it to be to suit their lifestyle - even in the Church!

"For the time will come when people will not tolerate sound doctrine and accurate instruction [that challenges them with God's truth]; but wanting to have their ears tickled [with something pleasing], they will accumulate for themselves [many] teachers to satisfy their own desires and to support the errors they hold." - 2 Timothy 4:3 (AMPC)

*Who do you say I am?*

I hear this as an invitation from the heart of Jesus.

**Selah...pause**

**Abide...**

who is He to you?

.........................................................................................................

.........................................................................................................

**Align...**

do I want to align with Him, His words and His truth?

.........................................................................................................

.........................................................................................................

**Apply...**

"If you openly declare that Jesus is Lord and believe in your
heart that God raised Him from the dead, you will be saved.
For it is by believing in your heart that you are made right
with God, and it is by openly declaring your faith that you
are saved" - Romans 10:9-10

.........................................................................................................

.........................................................................................................

Thank You, Lord, for the invitation to acknowledge You and love You. If I live by the truth of Your Word, You build my life on the rock of who You are. No power from hell can overcome me or Your Church!

God has highly exalted Him and bestowed on Him the name which is above every name. So that at the name of Jesus EVERY KNEE SHALL BOW.

Philippians 2:9-10 (AMPC)

Jesus said to him, "I am the only Way to God and the real Truth and the real Life."

John 14:6 (AMPC)

# He shall
# be called...
# Wonderful.

Isaiah 9:6

# Day 14

*Wonderful*

The Hebrew word translated as 'Wonderful' is 'pala' meaning wondrous, marvellous and miraculous, something surpassing and special and extraordinary, beyond our power and understanding.

"O Lord my God, You have performed many wonders for us.
    Your plans for us are too numerous to list.
    You have no equal.
If I tried to recite all Your wonderful deeds,
    I would never come to the end of them."
- Psalm 40:5

*You have no equal!*

Well Jesus certainly has no equal! No one can match His wonders! He came from the glorious presence of God to His people because of His covenant love, mercy and faithfulness to them. He made the way for everyone to come into salvation and freedom through His victorious death. He is the Way, the Truth and the Life with all authority and power forever!

What wonderful hope where there was despair and a future where there was none - beautiful!

"Those who have been ransomed by the Lord will return.
   They will enter Jerusalem singing,
   crowned with everlasting joy.
Sorrow and mourning will disappear,
   and they will be filled with joy and gladness.
'I, yes I, am the one who comforts you.'"
- Isaiah 51:11-12

This is the most tender love and undeserved mercy!

"At the very moment I called out to You, You answered me. You strengthened me deep within my soul and breathed fresh courage into me." - Psalm 138:3 (TPT)

These are some of the most beautiful verses in scripture of His wonderful love and reign in us now.

"If God is for us, who can ever be against us? Since He did not spare even His own Son but gave Him up for us all, won't He also give us everything else? Who dares accuse us whom God has chosen for His own? No one—for God Himself has given us right standing with Himself. Who then will condemn us? No one—for Christ Jesus died for us and was raised to life for us, and He is sitting in the place of honour at God's right hand, pleading for us.

"Can anything ever separate us from Christ's love? Does it mean He no longer loves us if we have trouble or calamity, or are persecuted, or hungry, or destitute, or in danger, or threatened with death?...No, despite all these things, overwhelming victory is ours through Christ, who loved us.

"And I am convinced that nothing can ever separate us from God's love. Neither death nor life, neither angels nor demons, neither our fears for today nor our worries about tomorrow— not even the powers of hell can separate us from God's love. No power in the sky above or in the earth below—indeed, nothing in all creation will ever be able to separate us from the love of God that is revealed in Christ Jesus our Lord." - Romans 8:31-39.

*May we never lose our wonder.*

**Selah...pause**

**Abide...**
*my heart has heard you say 'come.'*

........................................................................................

........................................................................................

........................................................................................

**Align...**
*with the truth that there is no condemnation or separation from Him.*

........................................................................................

........................................................................................

........................................................................................

**Apply...**
*ask Him to fill you with comfort and wonder at all that He has done.*

........................................................................................

........................................................................................

........................................................................................

Thank you, Lord. I worship You. May I never lose my wonder.

We love Him
because He
first loved us.

1 John 4:19

*Satisfy us each morning with Your unfailing love, so we may sing for joy to the end of our lives.*

Psalm 90:14

He shall
be called...
Counsellor.

Isaiah 9:6

# Day 15

## Counsellor

Before Jesus died and ascended, He had promised to His disciples that He would send "another" helper to be with them.

"And I will ask the Father, and He will give you another Comforter, Counsellor, Helper, Intercessor, Advocate, Strengthener, and Standby, that He may remain with you forever, the Spirit of Truth...for He lives with you [constantly] and will be in you." - John 14:16-17 (AMPC)

In Israel's history, the Holy Spirit had come upon men and women of God to speak His Word or work acts of power on His behalf, but this was the outpouring of the Holy Spirit that would be dwelling in believers.

"Fifty days after Jesus had ascended the disciples were all together in one place. Suddenly a sound like the blowing of a violent wind came from heaven and filled the whole house where they were sitting. They saw what seemed to be tongues of fire that separated and came to rest on each of them. All of them were filled with the Holy Spirit and began to speak in other tongues as the Spirit enabled them."
- Acts 2:1-4 (ESV)

The Holy Spirit is the Spirit of Jesus. He came to fill the believers with His presence, His power, His words, His prayer language He strengthened the believers to live for Him in boldness and courage, and displayed God's miracles for those around them. We can have this same Holy Spirit presence, He is the Wonderful Counsellor now in us. The Holy Spirit is the seal of our salvation, He is the guarantee of our future life in the Kingdom to come!

"And the Spirit of the Lord will rest on Him—
    the Spirit of wisdom and understanding,
the Spirit of counsel and might,
    the Spirit of knowledge and the fear of the Lord.
He will delight in obeying the Lord."
- Isaiah 11:2

This is the Spirit of the Lord that comes to live in us leading us to obedience. He is holy, He sets us apart as holy and teaches us the fear of the Lord. He leads us to truth as our thoughts and ways are so different to God's! He gives wisdom and revelation, understanding of His will and His ways. We listen to His leading and instruction, whether it's for personal instruction or for others. We need His counsel!

*"Lord, to whom shall we go?
You have the words of eternal life."*

John 6:88 (NIV)

Jesus is the Wonderful Counsellor! He made us, formed us, He is the one we need to turn to. He is wisdom. He is life. To whom else would we go?!

"We ask God to give you complete knowledge of His will and to give you spiritual wisdom and understanding. Then the way you live will always honour and please the Lord, and your lives will produce every kind of good fruit. All the while, you will grow as you learn to know God better and better." - Colossians 1:9-10.

"I will instruct you and teach you in the way you should go; I will counsel you with My loving eye on you." - Psalm 32:8

**Selah...pause**

**Abide...**

*You have the words of eternal life, to whom else would I go?*

........................................................................................................

........................................................................................................

**Align...**

*with the truth that when there is agreement and alignment with His Word, then our spirit, soul and body come together in peace and harmony.*

........................................................................................................

........................................................................................................

**Apply...**

*ask the Holy Spirit to come and live in you and know the truth that 'greater is He that is in you than he that is in the world' (1 John 4:4).*

........................................................................................................

........................................................................................................

Thank you, Lord, for not only guiding me with Your counsel but also sealing me as a guarantee for my future life with You.

The one who always
listens to Me will
live undisturbed in a
heavenly peace, free
from fear, confident and
courageous, you will rest
unafraid and sheltered
from the storms of life.

Proverbs 1:33 (TPT)

The meaning of My
words will release
within you revelation
for you to reign in
life!

Proverbs 8:6 (TPT)

He shall
be called...
Mighty God.

Isaiah 9:6

# Day 16
## Mighty God

"Christ is the image of the invisible God. He existed before anything was created and is supreme over all creation. For by Him all things were created that are in heaven and that are on earth, visible and invisible, whether thrones or dominions or principalities or powers. All things were created through Him and for Him. He existed before anything else and He holds all creation together." - Colossians 1:15-16

What an incredible scripture. Jesus was the Word that was spoken by God to create our universe and He holds it all together still by His Word! Jesus is the image of Almighty God, demonstrating God's power and might. He used His authority over storms, over sickness, over demons - even over sin and death. This same power is available to us!

"I also pray that you will understand the incredible greatness of God's power for us who believe Him. This is the same mighty power that raised Christ from the dead and seated Him in the place of honour at God's right hand in the heavenly realms. Now He is far above any ruler or authority or power or leader or anything else—not only in this world but also in the world to come. God has put all things under the authority of Christ and has made Him head over all things for the benefit of the Church. And the Church is His body; it is made full and complete by Christ, who fills all things everywhere with Himself." - Ephesians 1:19-23

*It is not enough to know about God, but to know Him!*

"...The people who know their God shall be strong, and carry out great exploits" - Daniel 11:32 (NKJV). There are works for us to do. His works that require our trust to step out in faith, knowing that Mighty God is in us! There are assignments, adventures, miracles to be worked. His authority has been given to us so that lives, families and communities can be changed.

*We need to know Him, but also who we are in Him!*

Paul prayed "that from His glorious, unlimited resources He will empower you with inner strength through His Spirit. Then Christ will make His home in your hearts as you trust in Him. Your roots will grow down into God's love and keep you strong. And may you have the power to understand, as all God's people should, how wide, how long, how high, and how deep His love is. May you experience the love of Christ, though it is too great to understand fully. Then you will be made complete with all the fullness of life and power that comes from God. Now all glory to God, who is able, through His mighty power at work within us, to accomplish infinitely more than we might ask or think. Glory to Him in the Church and in Christ Jesus." - Ephesians 3:16-21

He is the unshakeable Rock in a world that's being shaken! "...Stand your ground on the evil day [of danger], and, having done all [the crisis demands], to stand [firmly in your place]. Stand therefore [hold your ground], having tightened the belt of truth." (Ephesians 6:13-14 AMPC)

When we spend time in His Word our roots go deep into Him, we get established in faith and we learn to stand firm. We can be a strength and encouragement to those around us. We can know the voice of God to have clear revelation of the days and the times that we are in to bring wisdom, understanding and strategies to those that need it. It could be for an individual or an entire community. This is our role in society! Living in the 'more than we can ask or imagine' because of His great power in us!

"The blessing that rests on the righteous
Releases strength and favour to the entire city."
- Proverbs 11:10 (TPT)

**Selah...pause**

Abide...
*in these amazing words and experience His love.*

..................................................................................

..................................................................................

Align...
*with the truth that His might in you means you can do mighty things; you make a difference!*

..................................................................................

..................................................................................

Apply...
*pray that you will grow in knowledge of Him and move out in His power to 'bless your city'!*

..................................................................................

..................................................................................

*Thank you, Lord, for 'more than I can ask or imagine' happening through me for Your glory.*

"I am the Alpha and the Omega – the beginning and the end," says the Lord God. "I am the One who is, who always was, and who is still to come – the Almighty One."

Revelation 1:18

*If God is for us,
who can be
against us?*

Romans 8:31

# He shall
# be called...
# Everlasting Father.

Isaiah 9:6

# Day 17
## Everlasting Father

The Father-heart of God is clearly seen in the Old Testament. God refers to Himself as a Father to Moses. "Then say to Pharaoh, 'This is what the Lord says: Israel is My firstborn son... Let My son go, so he may worship Me.'" - Exodus 4:22-23

God says through the prophet Jeremiah, "How gladly would I treat you like My children and give you a pleasant land, the most beautiful inheritance of any nation. I thought you would call Me 'Father' and not turn away from following Me." - Jeremiah 3:19 (NIV)

"'Is not Israel still My son, My darling child?' says the Lord... 'that's why I long for him and surely will have mercy on him.'" - Jeremiah 3:17.

The Amplified version for this verse says,

*"My affection is stirred and My heart yearns for him."*

These verses show the Father-heart of God yearning for His children. The same heart comes through in the New Testament.

Paul shares his own heart for his Jewish brothers to the Roman believers. "They are the people of Israel, chosen to be God's adopted children. God revealed His glory to them. He made covenants with them and gave them His law. He gave them the privilege of worshipping Him and receiving His wonderful promises. Abraham, Isaac, and Jacob are their ancestors, and Christ Himself was an Israelite as far as His human nature is concerned." - Romans 9:4-5

Paul went on to say: "God made salvation available to the Gentiles. But He wanted His own people to become jealous and claim it for themselves. Now if the Gentiles were enriched because the people of Israel turned down God's offer of salvation, think how much greater a blessing the world will share when they finally accept it...Yet they are still the people He loves because He chose their ancestors Abraham, Isaac, and Jacob. For God's gifts and His call can never be withdrawn." - Romans 11:11-12,28-29

Paul's heart yearned for his Jewish brothers knowing they were God's children and dearly loved! Jesus came with the same heart longing as His Father. He said of Himself, "I and My Father are one" (In John 14:9). He goes on to say, "Anyone who has seen Me has seen the Father!" He came to call His people to Himself and back into their Father-Son relationship.

"To all who did receive Him, who believed in His name, He gave the right to become children of God." - John 1:12 (ESV)

So if as a Gentile we have believed, we have been brought into the special relationship that was Israel's (Abraham's children). "And you Gentiles, who were branches from a wild olive tree, have been grafted in. So now you also receive the blessing God has promised Abraham and his children" - Romans 11:17. Amazing!

God loved us and chose us, "God decided in advance to adopt us into His own family by bringing us to Himself through Jesus Christ. This is what He wanted to do, and it gave Him great pleasure." - Ephesians 1:15

He is our Father and we are His children! The Holy Spirit who is in us will never leave us helpless or abandon us as orphans (John 14:18). "For all who are led by the Spirit of God are children of God. So you have not received a spirit that makes you fearful slaves. Instead, you received God's Spirit when He adopted you as His own children. Now we call Him, 'Abba,

Father.' For His Spirit joins with our spirit to affirm that we are God's children." - Romans 8:14-16

*We are no longer orphans!*

"As the Father has loved Me, so have I loved you. Now remain in My love." - John 15:9 (NIV)

Jesus tells us to remain in His love - the Father's love! Knowing His love, His affirmation, His approval of us brings us worth, and value that changes us at the core of our being. This love transforms and empowers us to live as children of God. This love is so needed in our broken and confused world where for many, knowing their true identity is a struggle.

A father's love is the greatest source of need in every human heart. The security and stability that Father-God's acceptance and approval brings far outweighs how our human fathers were - good or bad, amazing or absent.

All hearts need the everlasting Father's embrace.

**Selah...pause**

**Abide...**

*in Abba Father's love for you.*

...........................................................................................

...........................................................................................

**Align...**

*with the truth that you are a chosen, beloved child. Grafted into a wider family.*

...........................................................................................

...........................................................................................

**Apply...**

*ask the Father to heal your heart, to fill you with His love and reassure you that you are not an orphan.*

...........................................................................................

...........................................................................................

*Thank you Father, Son and Holy Spirit that I have been adopted into Your family - You will never leave me!*

See what great
love the Father has
lavished on us, that
we should be called
children of God! And
that is what we are.

1 John 3:1 (NIV)

My father and mother abandoned me... I was like an orphan. But You took me in and made me Yours... You became my home, my place of settled peace.

Psalm 27:10 (TPT)

He shall
be called...
Prince of Peace.

Isaiah 9:6

# Day 18

## Prince of Peace

God is a God of covenant. He keeps His Word. "'For the mountains may depart and the hills be removed, but My steadfast love shall not depart from you, and My covenant of peace shall not be removed,' says the Lord, who has compassion on you." - Isaiah 54:10 (ESV)

God wanted His people to live in His peace. He had told the priests to speak this special blessing over His people.

"The Lord bless you
    and keep you;
the Lord make His face shine on you
    and be gracious to you;
the Lord turn His face toward you

and give you peace."
- Numbers 6:24-26 (NIV)

They were to live knowing that His wonderful favour and face - His smile - was towards them! To know His grace and protection over them. To have His complete Shalom - His fullness of life and tranquillity. This is peace!

Wow! God's people were apart from Him because of sin but, because He is a God of covenant, He sent the Messiah who is the Prince of Peace; Sar Shalom (Hebrew). He is the ruler who is peace. He is the source of all peace.

Shalom is harmony, wholeness, health, completeness, prosperity, welfare and tranquillity, nothing lacking, nothing missing! Just think about these amazing words.

Jesus, the Prince of Peace, came and reconciled us back to God through His blood. Being forgiven by God brings His Peace. There is nothing like this peace! It's an internal stillness. The Prince of Peace doesn't just give peace - He is peace!

When His reign of peace is in us, it settles our whole being - it is well, even when we face difficult situations, circumstances or people! Life can be challenging but He gives us the peace of God, which transcends all understanding and guards our hearts and minds in Christ Jesus (Philippians 4:7).

# It is well!

How wonderful that our hearts and minds can be at peace even in the middle of the shakings that the world is going through. When we are anxious and fearful, we go to Jesus and pray. We read the Word of God and let Him speak peace to our thoughts and emotions! Keeping our mind fixed on Him, focused and stilled through His Word and Spirit, brings freedom from agitation!

"You will keep him in perfect peace whose mind is stayed on You, because he trusts in You" - Isaiah 26:3 (ESV). This is amazing and it's true!

"Let God transform you into a new person by changing the way you think. Then you will learn to know God's will for you, which is good and pleasing and perfect." - Romans 12:2

He wants to change the way we think and deal with issues that cause agitation. He renews our minds when He speaks to us and shows us Himself. We learn that His way is pleasing and perfect for us and we can live free from stress and anxiety that plagues our hearts and minds. This peace can then bring freedom from distress and dis-ease in our souls, which can then bring healing of disease in our bodies! This is life as God intended it!

"Surrender your anxiety. Be still and realise [know] that I am

God. I am God above all the nations, and I am exalted throughout the whole earth. Here He stands! The Commander!" - Psalm 46:10-11 (TPT)

Knowing that the Prince of Peace is in control gives us peace. We can have freedom from fear as His "perfect love casts out all fear" (1 John 4:18). We can face any situation because we know that Jesus has overcome the world and we can trust Him, we are secure. We can also trust Him with our loved ones. He loves them more than we do. When we entrust them into His arms, we can know they are secure too!

Jesus said "Peace I leave with you, My peace I give to you; not as the world gives do I give to you. Let not your heart be troubled, neither let it be afraid." - John 14:27

*Shalom peace is 'untroubled, undisturbed, well being.'* - Philippians 4:9 AMPC

**Selah...pause**

**Abide...**

*be still and know that I am God.*

........................................................................................................

........................................................................................................

**Align...**

*bring every anxious thought to Him and ask Him where you are troubled and disturbed.*

........................................................................................................

........................................................................................................

**Apply...**

*ask the Prince of Peace to remove agitation and anxiety and fill you with His Shalom.*

........................................................................................................

........................................................................................................

*Thank you, Lord, that You make me complete through Your shalom, harmony, wholeness, health, completeness, prosperity, welfare and tranquillity, nothing lacking, nothing missing!*

Now may the Lord
of peace Himself give
you peace always
in every way.

2 Thessalonians 3:16

Now, because of You
Lord, I will lie down
in peace and sleep
comes at once, for no
matter what happens,
I will live unafraid!

Psalm 4:8 (TPT)

Of the increase
of His government
and peace there
shall be no end.

Isaiah 9:7 (ESV)

# Day 19

## His Government & Peace

The Messiah, the Prince of Peace, came to bring peace and His governance, His Kingdom rule and reign forever. It is continually increasing. For those who believe, when they live a yielded life daily going to God in prayer, worship, reading the Word and obedience to His leading, then His nature and His character will change them. His ways and His authority will work through their lives, affecting situations and lives around them with His Kingdom.

The Kingdom of God is "righteousness, peace and joy in the Holy Spirit" - Romans 14:17 (NIV). He is in His people, outworking these things to bring change to homes, families, and communities! His nature of love, joy, peace, patience, goodness, kindness, faithfulness, gentleness and self control

(Galatians 5:22) are also being outworked in lives, so they reflect God's heart of justice and mercy in this world.

The Prince of Peace restores lives and broken relationships so we can live at peace with one another. Conflict happens through sin in people's lives that wages war in them and then affects others.

"What is causing the quarrels and fights among you? Don't they come from the evil desires at war within you? You want what you don't have, so you scheme and kill to get it. You are jealous of what others have, but you can't get it, so you fight and wage war to take it away from them." - James 4:1-2

As we are reconciled with God, we can be reconciled to others and we can then become ministers of reconciliation (2 Corinthians 5:18). He enables us to live in humility and unity with others. This is His governance and rule and reign increasing in and advancing through His people.

"For Christ Himself has brought peace to us. He united Jews and Gentiles into one people when, in His own body on the cross, He broke down the wall of hostility that separated us. He did this by ending the system of law with its commandments and regulations. He made peace between Jews and Gentiles by creating in Himself one new people from the two groups. Together as one body, Christ reconciled both groups to God by means of His death on the cross, and our hostility toward each other was put to death...Now all of us can come to the Father through the same Holy Spirit because of what Christ has done for us...You are members of God's family." - Ephesians 2:14-16,18,19.

## Father God wants His family back!

We are forgiven and loved by Him, and we are called to forgive and love others. We can be peacemakers! Deep wounds of rejection and hostility between Jew and Gentile can be healed. Where there is recognition of one another's pain, where there is repentance and forgiveness, healing comes, then reconciliation and peace can follow. He knits us together in love as one new man; we stand together in unity.

We are no longer orphans fighting against one another out of jealousy, but the Father's love brings us together as brothers. We can be our brother's keeper where once we were enemies. This is a complete miracle and this is how He displays His wisdom and how He works His government and peace through His people together today.

Throughout scripture God worked through generational family life, bringing His authority, government and peace on the earth!

Together we are a Kingdom of priests, a people of a different spirit, and our unity and love as His Kingdom family affects change. As we overcome our differences and offences and align with one another we can pray and worship and work together to become a mighty force of love in the earth. Family is God's redemptive plan for all families, communities and nations!

**Selah...pause**

**Abide...**

in His love, joy, peace, patience, goodness, kindness, faithfulness, gentleness and self control toward you!

...................................................................................................

...................................................................................................

**Align...**

with the truth you are called to be a peacemaker and recognise any hostility in your heart.

...................................................................................................

...................................................................................................

**Apply...**

ask forgiveness of anyone you need to and be reconciled to anyone you need to be. Father God wants His family back!

...................................................................................................

...................................................................................................

Thank you, Lord, for Your government and peace in me and in my family. We live with generational blessings now.

"To be a Christian means to forgive the inexcusable because God has forgiven the inexcusable in you."

C.S. Lewis

The faithful lovers of God will inherit the earth and enjoy every promise of God's care, dwelling in peace forever. God-lovers make the best counsellors. Their words possess wisdom and are right and trustworthy. The ways of God are in their hearts and they won't swerve from the paths of steadfast righteousness.

Psalm 37:29-31 (TPT)

He will rule with
fairness and justice
from the throne of
His ancestor David
for all eternity.

Isaiah 9:7

# Day 20
## The Throne of David

David was king of Israel and his throne was in Jerusalem. God had promised him a descendant that would have an eternal reign over His people Israel and over His throne in Jerusalem forever.

"'For the time is coming,' says the Lord, 'when I will raise up a righteous descendant from King David's line. He will be a King who rules with wisdom. He will do what is just and right throughout the land and this will be His name: The Lord Is Our Righteousness.' In that day Judah will be saved, and Israel will live in safety." - Jeremiah 23:5-6

What a beautiful promise! We have seen through the cross, the Messiah established His righteousness in our lives. When we walk with Him as our Lord and Saviour, in His righteousness and live by the power of the Holy Spirit, we bring His nature and character and revelation of Him to others. We are His Kingdom of priests, a holy nation in the earth (Exodus 19:6).

However, the Messiah's Kingdom rule over ALL will only be established when He returns and takes the throne of David.

A day is coming when the nation of Israel will turn and call on God to save them and they will recognise Jesus as the Messiah and welcome Him as their King. He will come and will sit on the throne of David, on Mount Zion taking His place as their King and rule over the earth.

"My servant David will be their prince forever. And I will make a covenant of peace with them, an everlasting covenant. I will give them their land and increase their numbers, and I will put My Temple among them forever. I will make My home among them. I will be their God, and they will be My people. And when My Temple is among them forever, the nations will know that I am the Lord, who makes Israel holy." - Ezekiel 37:24-28

*A glorious day is coming!*

Jesus was born King of the Jews and He died King of the Jews. He will return to earth as King over all. The Messianic reign of the King will be over all the nations. They will finally recognise that He is Lord and submit to Him.

He will rule the whole earth with justice and fairness. What a wonderful covenant keeping God we have that will fulfil His Word. In the meantime we know the battle that rages around Jerusalem and God's purposes!

"Why do the nations rage
    and the peoples plot in vain?
The kings of the earth set themselves,
    and the rulers take counsel together,
    against the Lord and against His Anointed, saying,
'Let us burst their bonds apart
    and cast away their cords from us.'
He who sits in the heavens laughs;
    the Lord holds them in derision.
Then He will speak to them in His wrath,
    and terrify them in His fury, saying,
'As for Me, I have set My King
    on Zion, My holy hill.'
I will tell of the decree:
The Lord said to Me, 'You are My Son;
    today I have begotten You.
Ask of Me, and I will make the nations Your heritage,
    and the ends of the earth Your possession.
You shall break them with a rod of iron

and dash them in pieces like a potter's vessel.'
Now therefore, O kings, be wise;
  be warned, O rulers of the earth.
Serve the Lord with fear,
  and rejoice with trembling.
Kiss the Son,
  lest He be angry, and you perish in the way,
  for His wrath is quickly kindled.
Blessed are all who take refuge in Him."
- Psalm 2 (ESV)

As the nation's rage let us be those who align with the Son!

*Kiss the Son - honour Him.*

**Selah...pause**

**Abide...**

*kiss the Son, come before Him and honour Him.*

....................................................................................

....................................................................................

**Align...**

*with God's Word concerning Israel, the people and the place, as the nations rage.*

....................................................................................

....................................................................................

**Apply...**

*pray for the Church and nations to align with God, His Son - the Son of David.*

....................................................................................

....................................................................................

*Thank You, Lord, that I will rule and reign as part of Your Kingdom of priests in the earth.*

Stop your weeping!
Look! The Lion of
the Tribe of Judah,
the heir to David's
Throne, has won the
victory.

Revelation 5:5

"Wrong will be right, when
Aslan comes in sight, at the
sound of his roar, sorrows
will be no more, when he
bares his teeth, winter
meets its death, and when
he shakes his mane, we
shall have spring again."

C.S. Lewis

The passionate
commitment of the
Lord of Heaven's
Armies will make
this happen!

Isaiah 9:7

# Day 21

## *Zeal*

Zeal is defined as an eagerness and ardent interest in pursuit of something and it implies an energetic and unending pursuit of an aim or devotion to a cause.[5] The Hebrew word translated as zeal by some translations of this verse is 'qinah' and it speaks of the passion, ardour or the protective jealousy of a husband towards his wife. Its used over forty times in scripture and often describes God being excited to anger or executing judgement over His enemies.[6]

God is zealous! There was a zeal, a passionate commitment, in the heart of God for Him to move and act on behalf of His people and for the sake of His holy name as He is a God of covenant! Many scriptures speak of God being jealous and zealous for His people and His land.

"Shout this message for all to hear: 'This is what the Lord of Heaven's Armies says: My love for Jerusalem and Mount Zion is passionate and strong." - Zechariah 1:14

And again He declared: "My love for Mount Zion is passionate and strong; I am consumed with passion for Jerusalem!" - Zechariah 8:2

Judah and Jerusalem were created for His purposes; they are His people and it's His land. They have a purpose for all time for all mankind!

This is what God said regarding His people Israel: "Have you noticed what people are saying?—'The Lord chose Judah and Israel and then abandoned them!' They are sneering and saying that Israel is not worthy to be counted as a nation. But this is what the Lord says: 'I would no more reject My people than I would change My laws that govern night and day, earth and sky. I will never abandon the descendants of Jacob or David, My servant.'" - Jeremiah 33:24-26

There's no greater devotion or commitment than that!

And this is His promise concerning His Kingdom reign from Mount Zion, Jerusalem:

"Shout and rejoice, O beautiful Jerusalem, for I am coming to live among you. Many nations will join themselves to the

Lord on that day, and they, too, will be My people. I will live among you, and you will know that the Lord of Heaven's Armies sent Me to you. The land of Judah will be the Lord's special possession in the holy land, and He will once again choose Jerusalem to be His own city. Be silent before the Lord, all humanity, for He is springing into action from His holy dwelling." - Zechariah 2:10-13

"On this mountain He will destroy
  the shroud that enfolds all peoples,
the sheet that covers all nations;
  He will swallow up death forever.
The Sovereign Lord will wipe away the tears
  from all faces;
He will remove His people's disgrace
  from all the earth.
The Lord has spoken."
- Isaiah 25:7-8 (NIV)

This is our future hope and destiny! The kingdom of this world becoming the Kingdom of our Lord and of His Messiah, where He will reign for ever and ever (Revelation 11:15).

This is His passion! He willingly suffered for us all to redeem us to be with Him and we will rule and reign with Him forever with no more tears and no more death!

# This is the Passion of the Christ!

"At the cost of Your own blood You have purchased for God persons from every tribe, language, people, and nation. You have appointed them as a Kingdom and priests to serve our God, and they will reign on the earth." - Revelation 5:9-10 (NET)

Nothing can stop God's purposes and we are closer to that day than ever! May the same zeal for His purposes consume us. May our passion and devotion for Him cause us to live boldly proclaiming who He is. May zeal keep us living courageous and generous lives, reaching many with His love. May we be a fearless generation preparing the way of the Lord, until that glorious day when He comes to restore all things.

He who was, and is, and is to come is faithful.


**Selah...pause**

**Abide...**

in His passionate zeal and heart for you.

........................................................................................

........................................................................................

**Align...**

your heart and mind with God's will that He is working out
in the earth.

........................................................................................

........................................................................................

**Apply...**

pray for His zeal to consume you, that you live for His
purposes with boldness and courage.

........................................................................................

........................................................................................

Thank you, Lord, that Your passionate zeal consumes me to
reign in life with You.

Sing and rejoice, O daughter of Zion! For behold, I am coming and I will live among you. In that day many nations will join themselves to Adonai and they will be My people and I will dwell among you.

Zechariah 2:10-11

Behold, the dwelling of God is among men, and He shall tabernacle among them. They shall be His people, and God Himself shall be among them and be their God. He shall wipe away every tear from their eyes, and death shall be no more. Nor shall there be mourning or crying or pain any longer, for the former things have passed away.

Revelation 21:3-4

WE SAY
"COME"

# Notes

1 - Word Study: Reconciliation
https://www.simplybible.com/f654-word-study-reconciliation.htm
accessed 28/11/2023

2 - Oxford Dictionary
https://www.oed.com, accessed 28/11/2023

3 - Cambridge Dictionary
https://www.dictionary.cambridge.org, accessed 28/11/2023

4 - Got Questions
https://www.gotquestions.org/the-government-will-be-on-His-shoulders.
html, accessed 28/11/2023

5 - Merriam-Webster Dictionary
https://www.merriam-webster.com/dictionary/zeal, accessed 28/11/2023

6 - Bible Hub
https://biblehub.com/hebrew/7068.htm, accessed 28/11/2023
accessed 28/11/2023

 KingdomFaithchurch

For further information about Kingdom Faith Church and
other resources please visit: www.kingdomfaith.com
or contact us -

Tel:     +44 (0) 1293 851543
Email:  resources@kingdomfaith.com


Kingdom Faith Church is a UK registered charity (278746)